YOU CHOOSE

CAN YOU SURVIVE

BEING LOST AT SEA?

by Allison Lassieur

Consultant:
Howard Reichert, Member
Storm Trysail Foundation
Larchmont, New York

CAPSTONE PRESS
a capstone imprint

You Choose Books are published by Capstone Press,
1710 Roe Crest Drive, North Mankato, Minnesota 56003
www.capstonepub.com

Library of Congress Cataloging-in-Publication Data
Lassieur, Allison.
  Can you survive being lost at sea? : an interactive survival adventure / by Allison Lassieur.
     p. cm. (You choose survival).
  Includes bibliographical references and index.
  Summary: "Describes the fight for survival while being lost at sea"—Provided by publisher.
  ISBN 978-1-4296-6861-3 (library binding)
  ISBN 978-1-62065-711-9 (paperback)
  ISBN 978-1-4765-1808-4 (eBook PDF)
  1. Wilderness survival—Juvenile literature. 2. Survival at sea—Juvenile literature. I. Title.
  GV200.5.L27 2013
    613.6'9—dc23   2012027133

Editorial Credits
Angie Kaelberer, editor; Gene Bentdahl, designer; Wanda Winch, media researcher;
Jennifer Walker, production specialist

Photo Credits
Corbis: epa/Sujito Prakoso, 57, Mike Powell, cover; Dreamstime: Chris Harvey, 15, Willtu, 71; Rod Whigham, 19; Shutterstock: Alin Popescu, 105, AMA, 97, Anelina, 55, Arne Bramsen, 26, David Wingate, 36, doodle, 102, edella, 78, Eric Gevaert, 74, forbis, 84, Luisa Amare, 77, Marty Wakat, 61, PT Images, 90, RCPPHOTO, 41, Rich Carey, 6, rSnapshotPhotos, 12, Sebastian Duda, 8, Ventura, 44, vilainecrevette, 11; SuperStock, Inc: Minden Pictures, 49; Tami Oldham-Ashcraft, 43; U.S. Army Survival Manual FM 21-76, 33

Printed and bound in China.   005089

TABLE OF CONTENTS

About Your
ADVENTURE

YOU are sailing on the ocean when something suddenly goes wrong. You're at the mercy of storms, dehydration, and sharks. How will you stay alive?

In this book you'll deal with extreme survival situations. You'll explore how the knowledge you have and the choices you make can mean the difference between life and death.

Chapter One sets the scene. Then you choose which path to read. Follow the directions at the bottom of each page. The choices you make will change your outcome. After you finish one path, go back and read the others for new perspectives and more adventures.

YOU CHOOSE the path
you take through your adventure.

Sharp coral reefs
can sometimes cause
boat accidents.

CHAPTER 1

Danger at Sea

It happens in a blink—a freak wave, an unexpected accident, a fast-moving storm. Suddenly a pleasant day on the ocean turns into a nightmare of survival.

Of all the places in the world to be lost, the sea is the worst. At sea, there is no food, water, or shelter of any kind, other than what you manage to have with you. You're exposed to extreme heat and cold, as well as storms, waves, and wind. Most people who die at sea don't drown. They die of starvation, dehydration, or hypothermia.

It seems odd that you could die of thirst in a huge ocean of water. Ocean water is about three times saltier than your blood. That makes it impossible for your body to process safely.

Turn the page.

In case of emergency, the sail of a sailboat can be used for shelter from wind and rain.

A few swallows of saltwater will make you feel sick and vomit. More than that will causes seizures, brain damage, hallucinations, and death. Finding fresh water is necessary for survival.

The second most important thing, after finding fresh water, is protection from the elements.

The heat from the sun and the ocean winds will dehydrate you and make your skin burn, blister, and crack. Extra clothing, plastic tarps, rubber mats, life jackets, rugs, or even seaweed can help shield you.

A big problem for anyone lost at sea is hypothermia, which occurs when your core body temperature drops below 95 degrees Fahrenheit. You lose the most heat through your head, arms, legs, and groin. The best way to avoid hypothermia is to get out of the water.

Turn the page.

Water and shelter will keep you alive for a few days, but after that you'll have to find food. Anything edible will keep you alive, including fish, birds, and seaweed. But not all sea creatures are safe to eat. Puffer fish and jellyfish can be deadly. It's important to know which fish will keep you alive and which fish will poison you.

Even if the odds are in your favor, it's your will to live that will end up deciding your fate. If you have that, along with clear thinking and skill, it's likely you'll survive being lost at sea.

A jellyfish's sting is painful and can be deadly.

To be downed in a small aircraft at sea, turn to page 13.

To be adrift in a sailboat with a small crew in the Caribbean, turn to page 45.

To be lost at sea alone along the Atlantic coast, turn to page 79.

Small airplanes usually
have only one engine.

CHAPTER 2

Crash Landing

You walk across the small airport tarmac and take a look back at the evening sunset. You've spent the summer hiking, swimming, and relaxing with your family on this remote Canadian island. It's time for you to get back to school on the mainland, so you're leaving a few days early.

The small 10-seater airplane quickly fills up with other vacationers on their way home. You stash your backpack under the seat, strap on your seatbelt, and settle in. There's a sign overhead that says everyone must put on a life jacket. No one else has one on, so you don't bother. You doze off, barely feeling the plane taxi down the runway and lift into the sky.

Turn the page.

A shaking sensation wakes you. You're horrified to realize that it's the plane that's shaking. Your heart hammers in your chest, but you try to stay calm. Miles of ocean stretch below with no land in sight. The engine makes a loud coughing sound as the plane continues to drop. The water is getting closer. You hear the pilot, Sam, over the intercom.

"We're going to hit, folks. Brace yourselves."

You put your head between your knees, grasping your legs with your arms. Everyone else does the same. The plane's engine whines loudly, and then you hear a loud explosion. Something hits the back of your head, knocking you unconscious.

You wake up minutes later. The plane is in the ocean, broken into sections. The part you're in is sinking fast. Your head is throbbing from the injury. Sputtering as you swallow the cold water, you flip the seat belt buckle and swim free.

Then you remember your backpack. There's a bottle of water, some trail mix, your wallet, and a wad of dirty clothes inside.

The water is one of the most dangerous places for a plane to crash.

To look for your backpack, turn to page **16**.

To leave it behind and swim away from the wreckage, turn to page **19**.

You don't have to search long. The backpack
is floating a few feet away. You wrap one strap
around your wrist and swim away from the
plane's wreckage.

The choppy waves make you feel sick to your
stomach. A large chunk of the plane floats past, and
you manage to grab it. This is good—staying afloat
is key to survival. Too bad you didn't grab your life
jacket when you had the chance.

A familiar smell stings your nose and burns your
throat. Fuel! It must be leaking out of the airplane.
If it catches fire, you're in trouble. But you want to
stay close to the plane to salvage anything useful
and find any other survivors.

*To swim clear of the fuel, go to page **17**.*

*To stay with the plane, turn to page **32**.*

Taking a deep breath, you dip your head beneath the water and swim away from the fuel slick. When you come up for air, you're clear. By now it's almost dark.

"Help me!" someone shouts from somewhere in front of you.

Sure enough, you see a dark figure waving his arms. He goes under the waves and then comes up, sputtering.

"Help!" he cries again, but it's much fainter. He's drowning. Drowning people are dangerous. In their panic, they could drown anyone trying to rescue them. You have to be careful about how you approach him.

To swim around behind him, turn to page 18.

To swim directly to the drowning man, turn to page 33.

You swim around and surface behind the man. As he goes under, you pull him up by the hair, ducking his flailing arms. Grabbing him under the armpits, you swim backward, pulling his face out of the water. He's coughing and vomiting, but he's alive. After a few strokes you stop, exhausted. The man has relaxed. He says his name is Bill.

"Thanks," Bill gasps between gulps of air. "I can't believe I panicked like that."

Just then you both see a flashing light. Shouts ring out over the water.

"Is anyone out there?"

Together you start yelling as loudly as you can. A large rubber life raft looms out of the darkness. A life preserver lands near you both with a splash.

Turn to page 23.

You don't want to be near the plane when it sinks. You could get tangled in debris and pulled under. Slowly you swim out into the sea. You bump into something in the water. It's your backpack! A seat cushion is tangled in its straps.

You slide the backpack over your arm and grab the cushion to your chest. Then you pull your legs up. This position is called the Heat Escaping Lessening Posture, or HELP for short. But you can't hold that position for long. You stretch out in the water with the cushion tucked under your chin.

The HELP position helps conserve body heat in cold water.

Turn the page.

You have no idea how long you've been in the water, but it's probably no more than an hour. You're lightheaded from your head injury. All the seawater you've swallowed comes up in a wave of nausea. It's hard to think clearly. Becoming disoriented and having hallucinations are symptoms of hypothermia, but you don't feel that cold. Besides, it's still summer.

You feel sleepy, but you shake yourself awake. You need to move to warm your muscles. From somewhere you remember that moving is bad because it uses more body heat than being still. But to your confused mind, that doesn't seem right.

To remain still, go to page 21.

To get moving to stay warm, turn to page 34.

Slowly, painfully, you pull your knees back into your chest and float upright. You fight to stay conscious, but your thoughts are jumbled and don't make any sense. You remember a grizzly bear you saw on vacation. Suddenly there it is, in the water in front of you!

"Are you OK?" the bear says. Then the bear starts shaking you—hard. You take a swing at it, and then the fog lifts from your mind. The bear turns into a man hanging onto a large piece of debris.

"I guess not," you reply shakily. "I thought you were a bear."

The man chokes out a laugh. "Hypothermia. We need to get you out of the water."

Turn the page.

The man tells you his name is Bill. He swims behind you and helps you scramble onto a piece of debris. The air feels freezing, but you know it's warmer than the water. You lie there, teeth chattering, until you notice a flashing light not too far away. At first you think it's another hallucination. Then it flashes again. In the brief flash of light, you see a large rubber raft inching toward you. "Help! Help!" you and Bill cry.

Strong hands lift you out of the water. You're wrapped in something dry and warm. Someone presses a plastic water bottle to your lips. You drink thirstily. Then someone opens your mouth and presses a pill under your tongue.

"For seasickness," a voice you recognize says. "Let it dissolve."

It's Sam, the pilot!

"I'm glad to see you," you say.

"Good to see you too," Sam replies, examining your head wound. "I don't think this is too bad," he says, popping open a first-aid kit. He wipes away the caked blood with an antiseptic pad.

Now that you're out of the water and hydrated, you're feeling much better. Bill and two other survivors huddle in blankets in the raft. With you and Sam, that makes five survivors. Six are still missing.

Turn the page.

"We found five who didn't make it," Sam says sadly. "There's only one more." After you strap on a life jacket, Sam hands you a flashlight. Together you sweep the ocean and debris looking for the other passenger.

Your flashlight moves over a bit of bright red fabric. A jacket—and someone's in it. "There!" you say. The figure lifts her head weakly.

"She's floating!" you yell. The woman is doing the dead man's float to conserve her energy.

Sam throws the life preserver, which is attached to a rope, into the water. The woman tries to grab the preserver, but she can't move her arms well. She tries again and misses. A wave pushes her farther out.

"I'll go get her," you say, jumping into the water before Sam can protest.

To grab the life preserver first, go to page **25**.

To swim out to the woman, turn to page **35**.

As you swim toward the woman, you grab the rope that's attached to the life preserver and follow it out. When you get to the woman, she's not moving.

"Grab the life preserver!" you say, pushing it to her. She lifts one arm, and then lets it fall weakly back into the water.

"You can do this," you shout. "Don't die here!" Being careful to not get too close, you put her hands on the life preserver. She revives and clutches it to her chest in a tight grip.

"That's it," you say. "Hang on, and we'll be in the raft in no time."

Sam pulls you both in, and you immediately wrap her in a blanket and give her water.

"Thanks," the woman says. "I'm Emma." You'd like to tell her everything's going to be OK, but you're not sure that's true.

Turn the page.

A tarp and a rope are important tools for sea survival.

When Emma is comfortable, you approach Sam. "Is help coming?" you ask quietly.

"I hope so," he says. "We were off course when the plane crashed, so it might be a few hours. When it's light, we need to take an inventory of supplies and build an anchor so we don't drift."

Curling up under a blanket, you try to get some sleep. The rising sun wakes you. You're terribly thirsty and still nauseous, but alive. So far.

To inventory the supplies, go to page **27**.

To build the anchor, turn to page **36**.

You take note of everything in the raft. There's a small pile of salvaged stuff, including a few seat cushions, clothing, a small cooler, a couple of plastic jugs, and a broken mirror. The cooler contains several soggy sandwiches, a few cans of soda, some water, and a jar of olives. You give Sam a jug to fill with ocean water for an anchor. You also show him what's in your backpack.

"The extra clothing will be good protection," he says. The raft kit contains a plastic tarp, emergency rations, three gallons of fresh water, the thermal blankets that Sam gave out, and a two-way radio. You get excited when you find the radio, but Sam shakes his head.

"Not working," he says. "The crash must have broken it. I'm sure we'll be rescued within the next 24 hours, but we should figure out the rations for a week." Even with the water and trail mix from your backpack, there isn't enough for six people.

Turn the page.

"Don't worry, it'll keep us alive," Sam says. "A person can survive on four ounces of water a day. It won't be fun, though."

By now the sun is high in the sky. The other passengers are stirring. Together you and Sam divide the rations so that everyone will have food and water for seven days. Then you pass out the day's rations to everyone.

"Don't drink your water ration today if you can help it," Sam says. "Right now, we have plenty of water in our systems. We'll need this water later in case …" He doesn't finish the sentence.

The day gets hot, so you all rig the plastic tarp over your heads to shield you from the sun. The sea is rough, and the raft plunges and dips in the waves. It's exhausting to hang on to keep from being flung overboard. The saltwater spray dries out your skin despite the tarps, and the heat is relentless.

You expect rescue any moment, but evening comes and you're still drifting. You've never felt so hungry and thirsty in your life. From the expressions on everyone else's faces, they feel the same way.

"Come on, Sam," says Bill. "The rescuers have to be on their way. Let us have the rest of the food and water."

"Yes, I'm sure we'll be rescued soon," says another man, Mike.

Sam is clearly uncomfortable. "It's not a good idea," he says.

"Let's have them," Mike says in a menacing tone.

Sam looks hard at the two men, and then silently passes out everyone's rations. They gobble and gulp hungrily, but you hesitate.

To eat your rations at once, turn to page **30**.

To save your food and water, turn to page **39**.

There's no way rescue isn't coming soon, you think as you eat all your food and drink most of the water. You feel full and comfortable for the first time since the crash. Everyone is in good spirits, and there's a lot of laughter and talk as evening comes.

The next day dawns bright. Everyone is still excited at the idea of rescue. As the day stretches on, though, conversation dies down. People try to nap under the tarp, and a few jump into the water to cool off. You know that's a bad idea because you need to conserve all your energy. Instead you dampen your clothing with a little seawater and put as many clothes on as you can stand. This cools you down and helps avoid heatstroke.

Staying still will conserve energy, and what better way to do that than to relax and sleep? You crawl under the tarp and try to nap. As the sun slips down on the horizon, your heart sinks. Another night at sea—and now with no food or water.

By morning everyone is half-crazed with thirst. You look at the sky, hoping to see rain clouds. If it rains, the tarp will catch the fresh water. But there's not a cloud in the blue sky.

Emma is the first one to drink ocean water. Mike, Bill, and the other survivor, Sarah, drink it too. Watching them gulp water makes you even thirstier. Seawater can make you sick at best, and kill you at worst. But if the rescuers are on their way, surely they'll be here long before the seawater can kill you.

To drink seawater, turn to page 38.

To wait longer before drinking, turn to page 42.

It's important to keep the fuel out of your eyes. You hold your head high above the water and kick toward a pile of debris near the plane's wing. It's almost dark, but you can see a seat cushion floating nearby. You grab it. Underneath the wing you see what looks like a blue cooler bobbing in the water. It could have food, water, or medical supplies inside.

Sparks pop and fly out from the wreckage. At first you think the loud WOOSH you hear is the ocean wind hitting your face. But the wind is hot, and the surface of the water around you bursts into flames. What's left of the plane explodes as a fireball of red flames and black smoke surrounds you. Lucky for you, the pain only lasts a few seconds before you sink beneath the ocean's surface for the last time.

THE END

To follow another path, turn to page 11.
To read the conclusion, turn to page 103.

"I'm coming!" you shout as you swim to the drowning man. Just as he goes under again, he grabs your shoulders and pushes you under in his panic. You let go of the backpack, trying to get away. He's strong, and he tries to climb on top of you, pushing you down farther. You're too exhausted to fight his strength, so you stop struggling. Both of you quickly sink to the bottom of the sea.

Rescue a drowning victim by throwing a floatable object to them.

THE END

To follow another path, turn to page 11.
To read the conclusion, turn to page 103.

It's hard to concentrate. In your confused state, you decide that it's foolish to stay in one place. Quickly you toss the backpack away and kick off your shoes, pants, and jacket. The water seems even warmer now that you're free of all those clothes.

From across the dark water you hear laughter and see lights. It must be a party on the plane, and they've started without you. "I'm coming!" you shout and start swimming. But the sounds keep moving around, and it's confusing. You swim one way, then another, but the water is choppy and you don't seem to get any closer to the party.

It's a lot easier to swim underwater, you realize happily. If you dive under, the waves will carry you right to the party. Without another thought, that's exactly what you do. You don't realize that you'll never make it back to the surface again.

THE END

To follow another path, turn to page 11.
To read the conclusion, turn to page 103.

The woman is alive but not moving. You unclip your life jacket and try to put it on her, but she's heavy and the waves are too strong. Finally you tie it around her chest.

As you turn to drag her back to the life raft, she revives and begins to scream. Panicked, she grabs you around the neck, pounding your wounded head. The force of the blows knock you out, and you sink under the dark waves.

THE END

To follow another path, turn to page 11.
To read the conclusion, turn to page 103.

Most life rafts inflate automatically and do not have a motor.

You need to figure out something that will create drag on the raft and prevent it from drifting too far away from the crash site. Sam gives you a length of rope, but what is there to use for the anchor? Looking around, you spot the cooler. After you tie the rope to the cooler, you and Sam throw it overboard. As it hits the water, the cooler comes untied.

Quickly you put on a life jacket. When you reach the cooler, you tie your knots correctly this time. As you start to swim back to the raft, you feel something tug lightly at your ankle. When you try to shake it off, it tightens around your leg.

You take a deep breath and dive underwater. Floating a few feet below you is a huge tangle of fish net, buoys, dead fish, and other debris. Somehow you managed to put your foot through a piece of the net. As you work on the jumble around your leg, the strong current catches the net and pulls it, taking you with it. You're dragged down so fast that you don't have time to be scared.

THE END

To follow another path, turn to page 11.
To read the conclusion, turn to page 103.

The salty ocean water tastes terrible, but it's cool and wet. You take tiny sips, hoping that it will keep you alive and not make you too sick.

It's not long before everyone starts vomiting. The raft fills with the smells and sounds of sickness. As the day goes on, some people drink more seawater. Some even drink their own urine, but they quickly vomit it up.

You vomit over the side of the raft and close your eyes. You never imagined your great summer island vacation would end like this. As you slip into unconsciousness, you hope rescuers will find your body so your family can give you a decent funeral.

THE END

To follow another path, turn to page 11.
To read the conclusion, turn to page 103.

It takes all your willpower to eat only one ration and stash the rest in your backpack. When no one is looking, you hide your backpack behind the seat cushions. Sam sees you and nods in agreement.

By the next afternoon everyone is desperately thirsty. Emma, the woman you rescued, wants to drink seawater. You and the others talk her out of it. "Let's try use the tarp to catch condensed dew overnight," Sam suggests.

You tie the tarp corners to the raft and weigh down the center with a plastic jug of seawater. Then you position the cooler underneath the tarp, below the jug. Your hope is that dew will run down the sides of the tarp and drip into the cooler.

There isn't any water in the cooler the next morning. Now no one can stop Emma. She takes huge gulps of seawater. Over the next few hours, the other passengers join her.

Turn the page.

You want to drink the saltwater so badly that you sit on your hands and bite your cracked lips to stop yourself. Sam puts a hand on your shoulder and smiles encouragingly.

It doesn't take long for everyone to start vomiting. They're not paying any attention to you, so you quietly eat a mouthful of food. Sam does the same. You curl into a ball and try to sleep, ignoring the moaning and vomiting.

When you wake up in the morning, the raft is bobbing lightly on the water. Then you realize that the raft is empty except for you and Sam. Frantically you rush to the side of the raft and scan the ocean for signs of anyone.

"They're all gone," Sam says through cracked lips. "The hallucinations from the cold and drinking saltwater got to them. Bill jumped first, then everyone else tried to save him."

You bow your head, filled with despair. You know that you and Sam can't survive much longer out here. Just then, you see something in the sky. Could it be? Yes, it's a helicopter!

"Look!" you shout, grabbing the piece of broken mirror. You angle it so that it flashes in the sunlight. Sam grabs the tarp and waves it with all the strength he has left. The helicopter turns and heads toward you! You can't believe your terrible ordeal is over.

The U.S. Coast Guard uses the HH-60J Jayhawk helicopter for search and rescue.

THE END

To follow another path, turn to page 11.
To read the conclusion, turn to page 103.

All around you, the other survivors are vomiting up seawater. Some people even drink their own urine, but that quickly comes back up as well. The inside of your dry mouth feels sticky. Your skin turns dry and shriveled, and you stop sweating. A dizzying headache throbs between your eyes. So this is what dehydration and starvation feel like.

Your thoughts are jumbled and confused, but somehow you hang onto the thought that "seawater is bad to drink." All your thoughts focus on that one idea, and you start mumbling it out loud. Somehow just saying it over and over makes things better.

Time seems to stop. You curl up in the bottom of the raft and repeat, "seawater is bad to drink" over and over. You don't even notice when Sam squeezes a few drops of fresh water into your cracked lips. Or the next day when several pairs of hands lift you in the air and load you into a rescue helicopter.

You wake up the next day in a hospital bed. The decision not to drink the saltwater helped you and Sam survive your ordeal. Sadly, the rest of the castaways weren't so lucky.

Real-life survivor Tami Oldham Ashcraft rationed her water supply while lost at sea.

THE END

To follow another path, turn to page 11.
To read the conclusion, turn to page 103.

Sailboats use the force of lift to move through the water.

CHAPTER 3

Adrift in Paradise

You can't believe you're here. Learning to scuba dive has always been your dream. You spent last winter taking lessons. Now you're on a chartered sailboat in the Caribbean with four other divers and the captain, Andy. It's the vacation of a lifetime.

When the boat left harbor three days ago, the ocean was clear and smooth. But now big clouds are gathering on the horizon. The water is choppy, but not too rough. Andy says he's gotten several reports saying the weather is fine. He's an experienced sailor. You're sure he knows what he's doing.

Everyone gathers to enjoy a delicious seafood meal. After dinner, you ask Andy about tomorrow's dive.

Turn the page.

"There's a beautiful section of coral reef I want to show you," he says. "But it's a few hours' sail away. We'll get there by morning if we do a night sail." He shows you a printout. "This is the latest news about the weather. There's a small storm in that area, but it should move through before we get there."

After more conversation, Andy says good night and goes to the wheelhouse. The other passengers say their good nights and go to their berths below the deck. You're not tired, but if you're going to spend all day tomorrow diving, you should probably join them.

To go to your bunk, go to page 47.

To stay on deck, turn to page 52.

It seems as if you've just fallen asleep when someone is shaking you.

"Get up!" It's Kat, one of the other divers. "We've got to get out of here!"

You jump out of your berth into several inches of water on the floor. The boat is rocking so hard that you lose your balance and fall. It must be really bad out there. You pull on a shirt and jeans. Over that, you put on your all-weather jacket. You could grab a few more things, but it might be better to head to the deck as fast as possible. Kat's disappeared. She's probably trying to wake the others.

To go straight to the deck, turn to page 48.

To collect a few belongings, turn to page 66.

Seconds may mean the difference between life and death. You head straight for the deck. You're halfway up the ladder when a huge wave hits the boat, sending it rolling. Fortunately your grip is strong, and you don't fall. You hear a yell behind you. It's Ben, one of the divers. The rushing water is pushing him back. You reach out for him, but the next wave throws him back. He disappears. It's all you can do to hang on yourself. "Ben!" you scream, but he doesn't reappear.

It takes all your strength to pull yourself up along the rail. Finally, you reach the deck. Flashes of sharp lightning streak across the dark sky. Wave after wave washes over the deck as everyone frantically tries to keep the boat upright. You can't tell who's who in the driving rain and darkness. There are two people near the tall mast. They're trying to get the sail down.

The storm must have come on fast if the sail was still up when it hit. Two figures move on the other side of the boat, near the area where the lifeboats are stored.

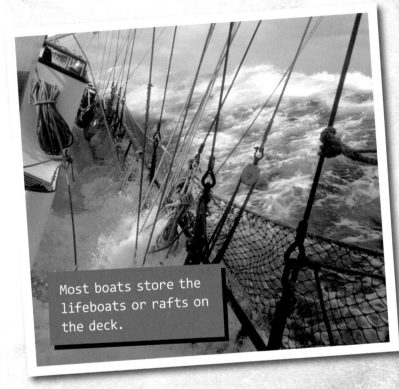

Most boats store the lifeboats or rafts on the deck.

To go to the lifeboats, turn to page **50**.

To try to help get the sail down, turn to page **67**.

Kat and another diver, Ian, are struggling with an inflatable lifeboat. It's so large that each time they try to get it into the water, the wind pulls it away. You grab one side, and together you manage to get it upright. As you try to drop the boat overboard, a wave washes over the deck. It rips the lifeboat from everyone's grasp. In an instant it's gone.

Ian pulls you to the back of the boat, where a small inflatable raft is usually tied. It's the raft the divers used each day to get out to the coral reefs. There's no way it could still be there in this storm! You're shocked to see it in the water, upside down.

With a sickening screech of wood and metal, the boat begins to tear apart. Ian grabs the rope tethering the raft to the boat and jumps into the water, followed by Kat. You grab the rope and jump too. Somehow you manage not to let go of the rope when you hit the water. Moving hand-over-hand, you reach the raft and cling desperately to the side.

There's someone else in the water near the raft. Ben! Quickly he cuts the rope tying the raft to the sailboat. The raft shoots away on the crest of a wave, carrying all four of you with it.

You keep trying to get the raft upright. But every time, a wave comes and blows it back. Exhausted from battling the waves, you, Ben, Kat, and Ian cling to the raft, treading water and wondering what will happen next.

Turn to page **56.**

Night sailing is one of the best things about this trip. You lie on your back on the deck, marveling at the millions of stars in the sky. The gentle rocking motion of the boat lulls you to sleep.

A gust of wind awakens you. Choppy, rough waves rock the boat. A few raindrops are splashing the deck. The stars have disappeared, replaced by a blanket of clouds. It doesn't seem too bad, though. You remind yourself that Andy said there wasn't anything to worry about.

As the waves get rougher, you get more worried. No one is on deck, which means that everyone is likely still asleep. If you wake them and it's nothing, they'll all be angry with you. But if the weather turns bad, everyone will need to be alert.

*To let them sleep, go to page **53**.*

*To wake everyone up, turn to page **68**.*

If the captain isn't worried, you shouldn't be either. But it's getting too rough to stay on deck, so you make your way to your berth. You just settle in when you hear a sudden howl of the wind. The boat pitches hard, throwing you to the floor.

Grabbing your all-weather jacket, you dash out of your cabin. Water is pouring down the ladder. You bang on doors, yelling "Get up!" Kat and Ben are already dressed, but you have to shake Lisa awake. Ian isn't in his cabin.

The water in the boat is almost knee-deep and rising fast. Ben gets to the ladder first and grabs the rail. Then he pulls each of you through the rushing water and up the stairs. As soon as you reach the deck, a huge wave hits the boat. It's all you can do to hang on. Wave after wave throws the boat to one side, then another.

Turn the page.

Someone grabs you and pushes you toward the back of the boat. The small outboard raft the divers use to get to the shallow coral reefs is usually tied up here. It's gone, but you see a flash of white in the water below. It's the raft, swept off the deck and turned upside down.

You don't have time to wonder why there's no proper lifeboat as the sail above catches the wind. The mast twists like a corkscrew and breaks, falling to the deck with a crash of tangled ropes, cloth, and wood. Just before it hits, you jump into the raging ocean and manage to land near the raft. Ben's made it, and so have Kat and Ian. There's no sign of Lisa or Andy.

Ben saws with a small knife at the rope that tethers the raft to the boat. In a few minutes he cuts through the rope. Instantly the raft shoots out on the huge waves. You all try to turn the raft upright, but every time, a wave hits and turns it over again.

Everyone is exhausted from battling the waves and the raft. Finally, you all stop fighting the storm. You cling to the raft and tread water, hoping the storm will end soon.

Ocean storms can include swirling clouds and large waves.

Turn the page.

The storm rages for what seems like hours. But finally it dies down. The ocean calms as the rain tapers off. As the sky lightens with the dawn, you're horrified to see that the sailboat is gone. There isn't any debris on the water, either. Either the storm took everything, or the raft has drifted far away.

Ben and Kat appear to be OK. You've got scrapes and bruises but nothing serious. Everyone is cold and shivering as they cling to the raft. Even though the Caribbean water is about 76 degrees, it's still about 20 degrees lower than normal body temperature. You'll last longer in this water than in cold water before hypothermia sets in, but not that much longer.

Ian seems to be sleeping, so you paddle over and gently shake him.

"Ian, how are you doing?" you ask. He stares at you, confused.

In 2006 survivors of a ferry accident near Rebang, Indonesia, huddled in their life raft.

"Legs hurt," he says, and then puts his head back down. You tell the others that you think Ian's really hurt. All of you need to get out of the water.

To try to flip the boat, turn to page **58**.

To try to climb on top of the overturned raft, turn to page **70**.

The ocean is calm, so there's a good chance you'll be able to get the raft upright. Ben climbs onto the raft and stands up on one side. His body weight forces the other side to rise out of the water like a seesaw. Quickly Kat pushes the raft farther up, and they manage to flip it over. Ben and Kat climb in. They then help you haul Ian into the raft. You climb in last.

The extent of Ian's injuries shocks everyone. He has several deep cuts up and down his legs. Some of the cuts are already red and oozing pus. Red streaks run up his legs. He's got a fever.

"Infection," Ben says. "There's not much we can do." You wrap his cuts with socks and make him comfortable. Then you look around for anything that will keep you alive.

There is a layer of waterproof rubber on the bottom of the boat, which Ben pries off. "We can use this to keep the sun off us," he explains, rigging a makeshift roof over Ian. Everyone checks his or her pockets. You come up with half a bottle of water and some paperclips. Kat has a CD. Ben has his small knife and a half-eaten sandwich in a plastic bag.

"Let's wait," Ben says. "We can live off the water we already have in our bodies for a few hours at least."

The first day you don't do anything but curl up under the rubber roof and try to sleep. You must keep still and quiet to conserve energy. The sun is merciless. You and the others dip your clothing in the ocean and put it back on. You know this will help keep your body cool and avoid heatstroke. But you must make sure that everything is dry before the night brings colder temperatures.

Turn the page.

Ian is burning with fever and unresponsive. By morning he's dead. The three of you remove his clothes and gently slide his body into the sea. His pockets were empty, but all of you wash the blood and pus out of his clothing and divide it among you.

By now you're thirsty and starving, but no one wants to eat or drink yet. "Maybe we can catch some fish," you say, pulling a paper clip out of your pocket. You bend it into a hook and then unravel some of the thread from your shirt for a line.

"Don't handle the fishing line with your bare hands, and don't wrap it around your hands—it can cut you," Ben says, tearing off a small piece of the bread from his sandwich for bait. Nodding, you slip off your shirt and wrap it around your hand. Crossing your fingers, you lower your fishing line into the water.

Almost immediately you get a hit! You pull up a strange-looking fish with spots on its body and big, round eyes. Its face looks like a toad.

Some species of porcupine puffer fish are deadly to eat.

*To eat the fish, turn to page **62**.*

*To throw it back and try again, turn to page **63**.*

You're so hungry and thirsty that you can barely wait for Ben to slice the fish open before you start eating. It takes about half an hour before your mouth begins to tingle. You get so dizzy that you collapse, then vomit. Ben and Kat vomit over the side of the raft and start gasping for air. Your chest feels tight. It's hard to breathe. Your arms and legs start to go numb too.

You vaguely remember something about puffer fish being very poisonous. The toxin in their bodies causes paralysis and death. So that must be what this strange fish was. But it's too late now. The tightness in your chest gets worse, but you pass out before your heart stops beating.

THE END

To follow another path, turn to page 11.
To read the conclusion, turn to page 103.

It looks like a puffer fish, which are poisonous unless prepared carefully. You sigh and throw it back. The next time, you pull up a fish that looks more normal. None of you recognize it.

"Well," says Kat, "It's doesn't have pale, shiny gills or flabby skin. It doesn't smell bad. I guess it's OK to eat." The three of you tear into it, eating it raw. Ben breaks the spine and you suck the fresh liquid out of the bones. You even eat a fish eye, which is a great source of water.

You pull off small bits of fish for bait. After an hour or so, you have several more fish lying in the raft. Ben slices the few remaining pieces of fish and lays them out to dry. You'll use them for food and bait tomorrow.

Turn the page.

"I wonder where we are," you say. You see a group of sea birds flying in the distance. Ben sees them too. Then you both notice seaweed floating in the water.

"Hey, we must be close to land," Ben says excitedly. "Birds and seaweed are clues." You grab as much seaweed as you can reach. Seaweed is a warm covering—plus, you can eat it.

"We could follow the birds," Kat says. "We can paddle the boat with our hands and take turns swimming and pulling the raft."

To take turns pulling the raft, go to page **65**.

To stay on the raft, turn to page **73**.

If there are birds and seaweed, land can't be too far away. You all watch the birds for a while, and you think you've figured out what direction they are flying from. That's where the land must be.

"I'm the strongest swimmer," Ben says. He ties the frayed raft rope around his waist and starts swimming in the direction of the birds. You take turns through the day pulling the raft until you see a small island far in the distance. You can't believe it!

As you get closer, you see white-capped waves crash against the shoreline. It doesn't look quite right, but you're exhausted. The fading light and your hunger must be playing tricks on your eyes.

To try to land here, turn to page 75.

To look for a beach, turn to page 76.

It'll only take a few seconds to grab your passport, some water, and some extra clothing. As you're digging through your duffle bag, the boat rocks sharply to the left. It sends you flying against the wall. Something in your arm pops, and a sharp pain sears through your shoulder. Screaming, you drop to your knees in the water. The roar of the ocean means the storm is hitting full force. You've got to move!

Painfully, you get up and stumble through the door toward the steep ladder to the deck. Before you reach it, a roar of ocean water cascades down the stairs and throws you backward. The last thing you see is the darkness of the sea as it covers you.

THE END

To follow another path, turn to page 11.
To read the conclusion, turn to page 103.

You slip and slide to the mast, hanging onto whatever you can to keep from going overboard. Andy and Lisa, another passenger, are there. The three of you pull at the sail, but it's no use. The winds are too strong. The sail billows outward in the wind, taking a tangle of ropes with it. The rope you're holding quickly knots around your legs.

As the sail whips out into the sea, it pulls you with it. You gasp as the heavy mast hits you in the chest. You're flung into the water, limp and lifeless.

THE END

To follow another path, turn to page 11.
To read the conclusion, turn to page 103.

Sure enough, everyone is angry with you for waking them. They're upset until Andy appears, holding a piece of paper.

"The storm has changed course," he says gravely. "Get on deck—I need everyone's help."

You've no sooner reached the deck than the storm hits. The light rain transforms into a raging downpour as huge waves rise and crash over the deck. The sail billows and twists crazily in the wind. Then the tall mast snaps, throwing sails, rope, and wood into the storm.

Everyone gets to the lifeboat. It takes every hand to get it upright and into the water. You all scramble aboard. The lifeboat rises and falls on the huge waves, and you vomit several times. But you're alive. You all huddle under the boat's plastic canopy, trying to stay as dry as possible. Eventually the wind dies down. The rain slows and then stops. You peek out from under the canopy.

The sky is getting lighter, so sunrise is near. There's no sign of the sailboat, not even any debris. It's a good thing you woke everyone up when you did. If you'd delayed only a few minutes, you all might be dead now.

The lifeboat is well stocked with emergency supplies. You pop a seasickness pill under your tongue and drink a bit of water. Andy shoots an emergency flare, followed by another a few minutes later. By midmorning a Coast Guard boat appears on the horizon. Your vacation might have been ruined, but now you can tell stories about surviving a storm at sea.

THE END

To follow another path, turn to page 11.
To read the conclusion, turn to page 103.

The three of you hoist Ian onto the raft. When his legs clear the water, you're shocked. Several deep gashes crisscross his calves and feet. A couple of them are red and oozing pus. Kat removes one of her socks and ties it around a wound. You and Ben do the same. It's not enough, but it's all you can do.

"Come on, we all need to get up there," Ben says, hauling himself onto the raft. But when you and Kat try to join him, the weight of all of you swamps the small raft. You and Ben quickly slide into the water.

For the next several hours you, Ben, and Kat take turns climbing onto the raft. Ian stays there, but he's developed a raging fever. He tosses and turns, muttering things that make no sense. You do what you can to make him comfortable, but he never regains consciousness. The next morning, you find that he's died. You and the others gently slide his body into the ocean.

It's your turn to be in the water. You put your jacket over your head to block the blazing sun. You doze off, but are awakened by something bumping your leg.

You try not to scream. The water is filled with sharks! You stop treading water and let your body float. Maybe the sharks won't bother you.

Blood in the water can provoke a shark attack.

Turn the page.

You stay as still as possible, letting your body float free. Ben and Kat slowly pull you up about halfway onto the overturned raft. It's all the weight the raft can handle, but you're grateful. Now you're only exposed to the sharks from your thighs down.

Closing your eyes, you try not to think about the circling sharks. Every now and then, something bumps your feet. Staying still is the hardest thing you've ever done. After about an hour, the sharks swim away.

As the sun begins to set, you hear the sound of a helicopter. Kat and Ben yell and wave their hands, but you don't have the strength to move. Suddenly there's a splash, and a man in an orange rescue suit is beside you. You and your friends are saved.

THE END

To follow another path, turn to page 11.
To read the conclusion, turn to page 103.

"We have no idea where land is," you argue. "Besides, we know we can survive on this raft. It'll only be a matter of time before someone finds us."

It's getting hot, so you all crawl under the rubber roof. You cover your exposed skin with wet seaweed and fall asleep immediately.

When you awake it's late afternoon. The others are still asleep. You stretch, trying to ignore your sunburned skin and the sea salt blisters on your hands and face. Looking up, you wonder if the birds are still here. Sure enough, you see one in the distance. But it's not a bird. It's a small airplane!

You dive for Kat's jacket and pull out the CD. Using it like mirror, you angle it until it reflects toward the airplane. Frantically you flick the CD back and forth, hoping the pilot will see the signal. At first you don't think the plane sees you. Then it roars overhead, dipping its wings back and forth. Yes! It flies away, but you know it saw you.

An hour later a Coast Guard boat appears. You, Ben, and Kat start cheering. Rescued at last! You only wish that Ian could have made it too.

A Dutch Coast Guard boat braves a storm to rescue stranded sailors.

THE END

To follow another path, turn to page 11.
To read the conclusion, turn to page 103.

Excitedly you all jump in the water and make the final push for land. The current tugs you, and then carries you forward with surprising strength. As you approach, the white-capped waves seem bigger and louder, and they're breaking farther from shore than you thought. It's not until you're on top of them that you realize that the waves are crashing against a line of sharp, deadly coral.

Before any of you can get away, the current pushes you into the small reef. The raft is sliced into shreds, and you feel as if a hundred knives are cutting you. The waves push you again, raking you over the coral reef and carrying you to the tiny shore beyond. You lay there, growing weaker as blood pours from the cuts. You made the wrong decision, and now it's going to cost you your life.

THE END

To follow another path, turn to page 11.
To read the conclusion, turn to page 103.

"I don't like the look of those waves," says Kat. "There might be rocks or coral there, which would slice us into a million pieces."

You turn the raft toward the end of the island and keep paddling. Finally, you spot a small white beach and aim for it. As you get closer, you see several figures appear out of the palm trees beyond the beach. They run into the surf and pull you to land. You lay on the warm sand, gasping and heaving, so relieved to be out of the water that you can't speak.

Your rescuers take the three of you to a large house nearby and give you food, water, and first aid. You tell them all about the storm, the accident, and your ordeal.

"Where are we?" you finally manage to ask.

Small islands dot much of the world's oceans.

"It's a privately owned island," one of the men responds. "Don't worry," he adds kindly. "You and your friends are safe now."

THE END

To follow another path, turn to page 11.
To read the conclusion, turn to page 103.

Some anglers use speedboats to fish in the ocean.

CHAPTER 4

Alone in the Ocean

There's nothing you love more than to take your dad's small motorboat out for a day of fishing off the coast of Maine, where your family is vacationing. Most of the time you like to fish with friends, but today you're thinking of going out alone.

You're an experienced boater and angler, but you've never gone out solo before. It's kind of exciting to think about being by yourself for a few hours. When you gather your fishing gear, you also remember to take some supplies. You pack sandwiches, fruit, and cookies in a cooler, along with a gallon of water. You bring a small radio to monitor the weather, a waterproof flashlight, and a flare gun.

Turn the page.

To be on the safe side, you grab an extra life jacket and an emergency thermal blanket. Just as you're going out the door, you spy some rope and toss that in as well.

In the boat are seat cushions, a plastic jug of gas, and a toolbox. The gas tank gauge says full, the anchor is securely connected to the rope, and everything is ready to go. You're out on the water before dawn. There are a couple of places you like to fish. One is only a few miles offshore. The better one is an hour's boat trip into the open ocean.

To stay close to land, go to page 81.

To go out to sea, turn to page 82.

You go just beyond the sight of land and anchor the boat. As the sun rises, you drop your line. The fish don't seem to be biting this morning. You love being on the water, so you don't mind. As the day wears on, the sky fills with clouds and the water becomes choppy. Flipping on the radio, you hear a weather report of a small storm. This doesn't worry you. Small, quick storms blow through all the time.

About noon, the fish start biting furiously. Most of them are too small to keep, so you spend most of your time throwing them back.

By late afternoon the clouds above have gotten darker, the wind has picked up, and the boat is bobbing furiously on the choppy water. But the weather report says the storm is passing to the east. You should be safe, but those clouds don't look good.

*To fish some more, turn to page **83**.*

*To go back in, turn to page **93**.*

The sun is just over the horizon when you reach your favorite fishing area. It doesn't disappoint you. In a couple of hours you have an impressive number of large fish.

As you unwrap a sandwich and open a soda, you remember another great fishing spot your uncle told you about. It's another hour out, though. Glancing at the sky, you see dark clouds in the distance. All you can get from the radio is static because you're too far out for a weather report. The last forecast you heard said it would be cloudy with some small storms. That shouldn't be anything to worry about.

To go farther out to sea, turn to page 85.

To stay put, turn to page 95.

The sky looks clearer to the north. Maybe you can get around the storm by heading that way. You yank on the anchor, but it's stuck on something. You pull until your arms hurt, but the anchor isn't budging. You could cut the rope, but then you'd lose the anchor. Maybe you can pull it up with the boat. The motor revs up instantly and the boat zooms forward. The front of the boat rises in the air, pulling the anchor rope tight. Quickly you shut off the motor, but it's too late. The rope snaps and the boat flips over, sending you and all your supplies into the ocean.

The water is freezing! You come up, sputtering. The waves and wind are getting stronger, and the sky is darkening. With a sickening feeling you realize that everyone was asleep when you left this morning. No one knows where you are.

Turn the page.

If you can get the boat upright, you may be able to get home. But the waves are so strong there's no guarantee that you can do that.

Small boats can flip and capsize easily during storms.

To stay in the water with the boat, turn to page 87.

To try to flip the boat over, turn to page 94.

You imagine the huge fish you'll catch in the new spot as the boat moves through the rough waves. It takes longer to get there than you thought. You drop your line, but the storm clouds are moving closer, and the waves kick up. A gust of chilly wind hits you. This was a bad idea. Stashing your gear, you turn for home, hoping to outrun the storm.

About 20 minutes later, the outboard motor sputters and chokes, then dies. The waves are much stronger and water is washing over the side of the boat. Frantically you check the motor and discover you're out of gas. Relief floods you as you grab the plastic gas jug. But the jug feels light, and it takes only a minute to see it's almost empty. You're sick to your stomach as you realize you didn't check it. You assumed the tank was full, so you didn't bother. You hurriedly pour the gas into the tank and continue on, even though you know you won't make it.

Turn the page.

Sure enough, the motor chokes and dies again. The wind is really strong now, and the waves toss the boat around like a bathtub toy. A huge wave catches you and sends you into the water. Another wave hits the boat and flips it over. Desperately you grab the boat and hang on.

The waves batter you and the overturned boat for what seems like hours. Then as fast as it appeared, the storm moves away. The sun comes out, and you're shocked to see that it's late afternoon. The storm only lasted an hour! You haven't been in the water as long as you thought. That makes your chance of survival much better.

The first thing to do is gather any supplies you can find. A few things are floating near the boat. But the waves are still strong, so you only have time to grab a few items before they're all washed out of reach. Once you have some supplies, then you can figure out what to do next.

To choose the seat cushion, the gas jug, and the thermal blanket, turn to page **88**.

To grab the cooler, the rope, and the waterproof flashlight, turn to page **91**.

You've lost the life jacket, but shoving the seat cushion under your jacket and zipping it up keeps you afloat. Using the thermal blanket, you tie the gas can to the boat, so it can't float away. You're too exhausted to try to get the boat upright. But you manage to climb on top of it. Now if you only had something to eat or drink.

The sunset is so beautiful that it almost makes you forget your dangerous situation. When the sun is down, the temperature turns much colder. The water is still choppy, and it takes all your strength to hang onto the boat. But you don't dare get back in the water and risk hypothermia.

Around midnight more storm clouds come, and the rain starts. Opening your mouth to catch it, you only manage to get a few drops. You need more.

To use the thermal blanket, go to page 89.

To catch rainwater with the gas can, turn to page 96.

Quickly you rinse out the jug with seawater. The thermal blanket is made from Mylar, a silver polyester substance. You roll it into a makeshift funnel. You stick the small end of the funnel into the jug. Immediately rainwater cascades into the jug. It works! By the time the rain stops, the jug is more than half full. That's enough water to keep you alive for several days, if needed.

At dawn you make more plans. Tearing a narrow strip from the thermal blanket, you tie the jug securely to the boat. A second strip of blanket will be a signal flag. You stretch the rest of the silver metallic thermal blanket over the boat. The sun is beating down, so you wet your clothing and put it all back on to keep your body temperature down. You crawl under the blanket, using the seat cushion as a pillow. Every time you wake up, you stand on the boat and wave the signal flag.

Turn the page.

At sunrise you're dizzy and desperately hungry. The cooler is long gone, but maybe there's something else to eat trapped under the boat. It might be safer to stay on the boat, though.

A thermal blanket works by deflecting body heat back to the source.

To stay on the boat, turn to page **97**.

To dive under and search for food, turn to page **98**.

Dropping the flashlight into the cooler, you tie the rope through the handle. You then strap it to the boat. There's a chance that you can turn the boat upright. For a time you watch the waves to see what direction they're moving. Then you push the boat so that it sits perpendicular to the direction of the waves. When you stand on one side and pull upward, the force of the waves pushes the boat even farther. It takes a few tries, but finally the boat is upright. You climb aboard and pull the cooler in with you.

No one knows where you are, you realize suddenly. Trying not to panic, you take stock of your situation. There's enough food and drinks to last a few days, if you ration it carefully. The boat seems to be in good shape. The flashlight is useless unless you need to signal at night. Halfheartedly you try the motor. As expected, it's not working.

Turn the page.

The sun is setting, and a gust of cool wind reminds you how cold it can get on the ocean after dark. With no blankets or coverings, all you can do is curl up in the bottom of the boat and stay out of the wind. It's too cold to get much sleep, but you manage to survive the night. For the next two days you sleep, eat and drink as little as possible, and scan the ocean and sky for signs of rescue. But you're alone.

By the fourth day your supplies are almost gone. You've seen several schools of fish swimming under the boat. But they're swimming too deep to catch. There must be something on the boat you can use to catch fish.

To try to make a hook, turn to page **100**.

To try to make a net, turn to page **101**.

The weather can be unpredictable, and you're not taking any chances. Just as you stash your fishing gear and start the motor, a huge wave hits the boat. You're almost thrown into the water, but manage to hang on. That was too close. The anchor seems to be caught on something, but a few tugs and it's free. Opening the engine full throttle, you speed for home.

The waves batter your boat. It's all you can do to bail out the water and keep moving in the right direction. The sky grows darker and the waves get stronger, but your little boat manages to stay on top of them. Finally you see land. You won't have any big fish to brag about, but at least you're alive.

THE END

To follow another path, turn to page 11.
To read the conclusion, turn to page 103.

You know how to flip a boat—get on top of it and stand on one edge, while pulling the other side up with a rope or a handle. Climbing onto the overturned boat is easy, but the waves and wind keep knocking the boat down.

Panicking, you keep trying. The sky grows darker, and flashes of lightning cut the sky above you. Sobbing in frustration and fear, you try again. But this time the wind catches the boat and hurls it sideways, hitting your head and knocking you into the water. You're unconscious as you slide under the waves.

THE END

To follow another path, turn to page 11.
To read the conclusion, turn to page 103.

Those clouds don't look good, but you have another couple of hours before you need to head for home. You're so intent on catching a big fish that you don't notice the sky darkening or that the waves are getting very rough. When a cold wave splashes into the boat, you realize what's happening. Quickly you store your gear and turn for home. From the look of those clouds, it's going to be close.

The waves get bigger and cold wind whips through you, but the boat stays afloat as you keep it pointed toward home. Just as the storm clouds open with torrents of rain, you reach the shore. Your dad is standing on the beach in the pouring rain, waving his arms at you. You've never been so glad to see someone in your life.

THE END

To follow another path, turn to page 11.
To read the conclusion, turn to page 103.

The gas can, of course! You rinse it out with seawater and then hold it up into the rain. By the time the rain stops you have about an inch of water in the jug.

By noon the next day you've drank all the water. No rain clouds are in sight. You slip into the water to cool off. You're so tired that you don't bother climbing back. But you've got to be out of the water and dry before nightfall. You pull the thermal blanket over your head and drift off to sleep.

When you wake up, the stars are out. There's a chilly wind blowing. Your mind feels sluggish and dull. The water is much warmer than the cold air. You can't remember why it was so important to get on the boat last night. You drift off to sleep again. You're dreaming of taking a warm bath as you sink below the surface of the water and drown.

THE END

To follow another path, turn to page 11.
To read the conclusion, turn to page 103.

Rescue crews use inflatable boats to search for shipwreck survivors.

You have to stay on the boat. Swallowing the last of the fresh water, you sit up and cover yourself with the thermal blanket. Every now and then you wave the signal flag. You pound on the boat, kick your legs—anything you can think of to keep moving and alert. You sing every song you remember, even the ABC song. When you hear the sound of a helicopter, you think you're hearing things. It's not until a man in an orange suit jumps into the water that you realize rescue has come.

THE END

To follow another path, turn to page 11.
To read the conclusion, turn to page 103.

The water is dark under the boat, and the first search turns up empty. On the third try, you find a plastic bag with your sandwich, fruit, and cookies. You eat the sandwich and wash it down with the rest of the water.

You decide to stay in the water through the heat of the day. A gust of wind blows the thermal blanket away from the boat. You reach for it but miss. It floats away. You lean against the side of the boat and doze off and on until the sun sets.

When you wake, it's hard to think clearly. You remember that you must get out of the water. Painfully you climb back onto the hull of the boat. It's freezing up here, and your soaked clothing makes it feel even colder. First you start shaking, but eventually that stops. Suddenly you have the urge to play basketball with your brother.

Hypothermia Chart

If the Water Temp. (F) is...	Exhaustion or Unconsciousness Sets In	Expected Time of Survival Is...
32.5	Less than 15 min.	Less than 15–45 min.
32.5–40	15–30 min.	30–90 min.
40–50	30–60 min.	1–3 hours
50–60	1–2 hours	1–6 hours
60–70	2–7 hours	2–40 hours
70–80	3–12 hours	3 hrs–indefinitely
more than 80	indefinitely	indefinitely

"Well, this is no place for some hoops," you think as you peel off your clothing. You're so far gone with hypothermia that you don't realize what you're doing. You dive into the water and start swimming for home. Of course, you never arrive.

THE END

To follow another path, turn to page 11.
To read the conclusion, turn to page 103.

After a few minutes of tinkering, you have a small pile of wires, springs, and coils. You bend a wire into a large hook and pull some strands out of the rope to use as a fishing line. Two cookies are left in the cooler. You use a piece of a cookie for bait.

For the next few hours you try to fish. It's becoming hard to concentrate, so you give up. You drink the last of the water and eat the remaining cookies.

By nightfall you are dizzy, disoriented, and so thirsty. Surely drinking a little seawater won't hurt. By morning, the vomiting starts. Somewhere in your dehydrated brain, you get the idea to fill the cooler up with saltwater and try to turn it into fresh water. You throw the cooler into the ocean and jump in after it. It's the last decision you ever make.

THE END

To follow another path, turn to page 11.
To read the conclusion, turn to page 103.

You tear your T-shirt open to form a large rectangle. Then you tie the corners together to one end of the rope. You lower it in the water and wait. A flash of silver means a school of fish has arrived. You pull your makeshift net through the fish. Finally you get the hang of it, throwing several small, flopping fish into the boat. You use a piece of wire from the motor to clean one of the fish and eat greedily. The eyes are good sources of liquid. You're so thirsty that eating them doesn't seem gross.

As it gets dark, you switch on the flashlight and shine it upward. Switching off the flashlight, you curl up in the boat and drift off. When the shaking starts, you try to push it away. It gets stronger, and you open your eyes. Someone has you by the shoulders. Then a woman's voice cuts through your foggy brain. "We saw your signal." You're rescued!

THE END

To follow another path, turn to page 11.
To read the conclusion, turn to page 103.

Severe storms can come up suddenly on the ocean.

CHAPTER 5

You CAN Survive

Water covers 75 percent of Earth's surface, and about 70 percent of that is ocean or sea. Most people will find themselves traveling on or above the water at some point in their lives. There is always the possibility that something might go wrong. Survival depends on your resourcefulness and ability to think and act quickly and rationally.

Most deaths at sea come from making bad choices and forgetting how powerful and dangerous the sea can be. The best way to survive is to keep your wits and to think clearly about what you're facing. Making the right decisions in the first minutes you're stranded in the water can mean the difference between living and dying. Knowing that most people lost at sea die of hypothermia, dehydration, or starvation is vital.

Even if you're just on the boat as a passenger, taking a sailing safety class before you go out on the water is a good idea. Then you'll be more prepared and less likely to panic during an emergency.

Being clear-headed about your immediate situation will keep you alive. You must be able to judge when to leave a boat in trouble, and when it's safer to ride out a storm. Get familiar with the boat. Where are the lifeboats and life jackets stored? Can you get to emergency supplies quickly? Can you radio for help?

If the worst happens and you find yourself lost at sea, you must remain calm and focused on staying alive. Is anyone injured? Do you have food and water? Are there other dangers nearby, such as sharks or coral reefs? Does anyone know where you are? Are you near land? The faster you understand the dangers you're facing, the better able you are to make a plan for survival.

Ultimately it's your will to live that will help you survive being lost at sea. If you focus on staying alive and not giving up, you have a much better chance of living through your ordeal.

Boats should carry a U.S. Coast Guard-approved life vest for each passenger.

REAL SURVIVORS

Yacht Wreck

Maurice and Maralyn Bailey's sea ordeal began when they set sail from Southampton, England, on their way to New Zealand. They sailed safely for several months until a whale destroyed their 31-foot yacht in March 1973. They salvaged some food, water, and supplies and escaped in a life raft. When the food ran out, they survived on rainwater and fish they caught using a bent safety pin. By the time they were rescued by a Korean fishing boat June 30, 1973, their clothing had rotted away, they had each lost about 40 pounds, and the lifeboat was falling apart.

Adrift in a Lifeboat

Steve Callahan was an experienced sailor and boat builder when he left Rhode Island on his small ship, bound for Antigua. In January 1982 his boat was severely damaged in a storm in the Atlantic Ocean. He managed to get onto a lifeboat with a sleeping bag and an emergency kit with food, flares, a spear gun, and solar stills that could produce water. He survived by eating fish, barnacles, and birds. When fishermen found him April 20, 1982, near the Caribbean island of Marie-Galante, he was dehydrated and covered with saltwater sores, but alive.

A Dangerous Swim

Late one September afternoon in 2008, Walt Marino and his 12-year-old son Christopher waded out to swim near Daytona Beach, Florida. They were caught in a riptide that carried them both out to sea. They survived by treading water, but after several hours the two were separated. As night fell, they stayed in contact by shouting "To infinity and beyond!" from the movie *Toy Story.* Fishermen rescued Walt the next morning. Christopher was found alive a few hours later.

Lost in a Dinghy

Three teenage boys set sail the night of October 5, 2010, from their South Pacific island home and ended up lost at sea for 50 days. The three boys, Filo Filo and Samuel Pelesa, 15, and Edward Nasau, 14, decided to sail from Atafu Atoll to an island 60 miles away. They collected coconuts and set out, but their 12-foot metal dinghy's motor eventually lost power, and they drifted out to sea. After the coconuts ran out, they drank rainwater they caught in a tarp and ate fish and birds. A fishing boat near Fiji—more than 750 miles away from their home—finally rescued them.

SURVIVAL QUIZ

You're in the middle of the ocean on a small sailboat when a storm hits. There's a lot of equipment on board, but you only have time to grab a few things before you get into the lifeboat. Which items will help you survive being lost at sea? Rank each of these items 1-10, from life saving to totally worthless.

- A. compass
- B. nylon rope
- C. extra water
- D. case of freeze-dried food
- E. floating seat cushion
- F. ocean maps
- G. fishing kit
- H. case of chocolate bars
- I. square plastic tarp
- J. shaving mirror

Source: Training Manager Success Strategies

Answers: C, J, D, I, H, G, B, E, F, A

READ MORE

Jeffrey, Gary. *Defying Death at Sea.* New York: Rosen Central, 2010.

Lassieur, Allison. *Can You Survive the Titanic?: An Interactive Survival Adventure.* Mankato, Minn.: Capstone Press, 2012.

O'Shei, Tim. *How to Survive Being Lost at Sea.* Mankato, Minn.: Capstone Press, 2009.

Ridley, Frances. *Lost at Sea.* New York: Crabtree Pub. Co., 2008.

INTERNET SITES

Use FactHound to find Internet sites related to this book. All of the sites on FactHound have been researched by our staff.

Visit *www.facthound.com*

Type in this code: 9781429668613

GLOSSARY

condensation (kahn-duhn-SAY-shuhn)—the process of turning water vapor into liquid

debris (duh-BREE)—the pieces of something that has been broken or destroyed

dehydration (dee-hye-DRAY-shuhn)—a life-threatening medical condition caused by a lack of water

hallucination (huh-loo-suh-NAY-shuhn)—something seen that isn't really there

hypothermia (hye-puh-THUR-mee-uh)—a life-threatening medical condition that can occur when a person's body temperature falls several degrees below normal

ration (RASH-uhn)—a specific amount of food, water, or supplies

salvage (SAL-vij)—to rescue property from a disaster

seizure (SEE-zhur)—a medical condition in which the body moves uncontrollably

thermal (THUR-muhl)—something that is designed to hold in body heat

BIBLIOGRAPHY

Callahan, Steven. *Adrift: Seventy-Six Days Lost at Sea*. Boston: Houghton Mifflin, 2002.

Colwell, Keith. *Sea Survival Handbook: The Complete Guide to Survival at Sea*. New York: Skyhorse Pub., 2009.

Kiley, Deborah Scaling, and Meg Noonan. *Albatross: A True Story of a Woman's Survival at Sea*. Boston: Houghton Mifflin, 1994.

Robertson, Dougal. *Sea Survival: A Manual*. New York: Praeger, 1975.

Schuyler, Nick. *Not Without Hope*. New York: William Morrow, 2010.

Wiseman, John. *SAS Survival Handbook: How to Survive in the Wild, in Any Climate, on Land or at Sea*. New York: HarperResource, 2004.

INDEX